This is a picture of me

My name is Meltem. I was born in 1993, in the little
village of Tilkiller, in Pazarcik in eastern Turkey.
We are Kurdish. My mum is called Cennet and my dad's
name was Yusuf. In Turkey, we lived on our pistachio
farm, which my dad looked after.

I lived a normal village life with my mum and dad.
I hadn't started school yet. My mum's parents
and my auntie, my mum's sister, were there too.

The Way Things Were – Pazarcik

Farm life was wonderful. Normal for us. Dad and my mum looked after the pistachio trees, and my mum used to keep the farm clean too. We also had lots of animals. Sheep, goats, horses, cows, chickens, and dogs and some donkeys. I loved it. We grew a lot of our own food too. And stuff we didn't grow we got from other people in the village.

MELTEM'S JOURNEY

A Refugee Diary

Anthony Robinson

Series Editor

Annemarie Young

Illustrated by June Allan

F
FRANCES LINCOLN
CHILDREN'S BOOKS

This is the true story of Meltem's journey, told in her own words. It follows her from her home village in eastern Turkey on an uncertain journey. First by coach to Istanbul, the capital of Turkey, then by plane to Koblenz in Germany, and finally to England, hidden in a lorry. She now lives in London with her mother, Cennet.

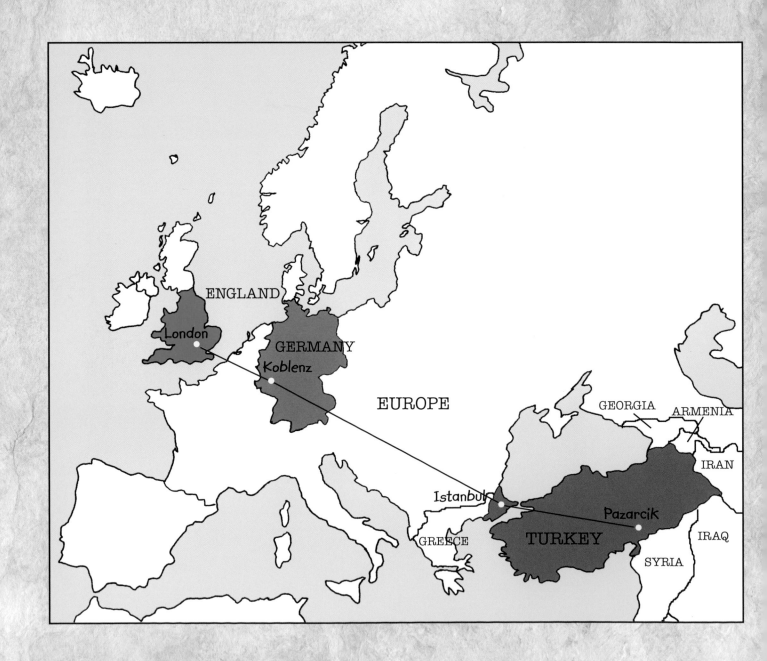

What I didn't know as a little kid was that the adults were scared of the Turkish soldiers. They would come and make trouble. There was nothing we could do about it. They were searching for weapons and things, or that's what they always said.

Everything Changes – 1999–2000

One day, in 1999, the soldiers came and beat my dad very badly. He had to have an operation. He left the village soon after. I was just five or six years old.

Dad didn't say where he was going. He just went. He had had enough I think. We heard months later when a friend rang and told us, that he was in Germany. He told us to go to him there.

Me and my mum left five months later, in spring 2000.
We went to Istanbul by coach and stayed for a couple
of days in a hotel.

We didn't wait too much. A man helped us get a plane to
Koblenz in Germany. My dad's brother was living there.
That's why Dad had gone there.

Koblenz, Germany – 2000–2001

Dad didn't meet us at the airport when we arrived. We applied for asylum, somewhere near the airport, and Dad came there. I don't remember a lot, I was too young.

Mum says German Social Services helped us then. Dad couldn't work while they sorted out our asylum application. The three of us lived in one room in a hostel. We shared a kitchen with about ten people. I remember it as dirty and there being lots of noisy dogs around.

I went to nursery there. That was OK. There were lots of other children. Some refugees and others. I had a Turkish friend there, but I don't remember her name. I used to like skipping with her. We played with Pokemon cards a lot too. At breaks and lunchtime we would go to the gym, for a rest. They would put a colourful cloth over us, even over our heads. It was nice.

One year later, in summer 2001, our asylum application was refused. We had to leave Germany or be sent back to Turkey. And we couldn't go back because my mum and dad would have been in big trouble for leaving illegally.

Leaving for the UK – 2001

We left pretty quick. A man arranged it for us and we got
a lorry late at night. I only remember it was dark.
My mum says we had to hide in the back of the lorry under
some stuff. The next day, 24 September, 2001, we arrived
in Dover. I remember it was daytime.

We asked for asylum straight away. The people there asked
us if we had come through another country, but we couldn't
say we had come from Germany or they would have sent
us back there. You have to come straight from your own
country to get asylum.

Then I made a big mistake by asking for sugar in German. Mum nipped me. The people heard and a woman came next to me and asked me and Dad a lot of questions. I got nipped by my mum again. I didn't understand why, but now I do.

We stayed in this office a long time. I think, in the end, they just gave up and stopped asking us questions.

They put us in a hostel outside London for about a month.

A Shock in Bradford – 2001–2002

The Home Office gave us a house in Bradford. We went there in a mini-van with some other families and stayed until early 2002. We'd wanted to stay in London, near my aunts and uncles and cousins, but we couldn't.

Bradford was bad for us. There was a lot of racism against us. We had our windows smashed and threats and stuff. And finally, they set fire to the front door of the house next door to us. It was empty, but our curtains caught fire. We had to call the fire brigade ourselves. Nobody else would. It was horrible. We went to the police then, and they gave us a letter saying it wasn't safe for us to live there.

I went to school there for a while too. I don't remember the name. It was OK. Not good, not bad.

We left a month after the fire business. We lived in Bradford for a few months altogether and it had been horrible. We were wondering when our lives would get better.

Mostly, Bradford is just a black memory.

Almost normal – Doncaster, 2002–2005

Then we moved to Doncaster, in spring 2002. That was the best place ever.

Doncaster was like a dream for me. It was just normal. I started school straight away, Stirling Primary School. I was eight and went into Year 3. Then in September I went into Year 4. It was normal because I had friends, went to school on my bike and just had fun. I never thought about being a refugee or any of that stuff. And I learned English in about three months. That was important for making friends and joining in.

But then our troubles started again. In late 2002
the Home Office discovered that we had come through
Germany. They put Dad into detention after he went to
sign in at the police station, like he did every week.
They took him to Manchester. This time he let us know
what was happening.

Mum and I then made our way to her sister who was
living in London. We stayed with her for a couple of weeks
until my dad got out on bail. Then we went back to our
house in Doncaster and life was normal again until 2005.

The Knock at the Door – April, 2005

Then it happened. On a Tuesday, at seven in the morning, in April 2005, they knocked on our door. They rushed us. Five security guards – four men and a woman. Someone shouted, "Pack your stuff. You're going back to Germany." We had twenty minutes to pack.

They took us to Yarl's Wood detention centre in Bedfordshire. Three days later they let us out because Dad signed a paper which said we would not ask for support. It meant we agreed to look after ourselves. At least we were out of that place. We got a solicitor then too.

But in the spring of 2006 we were told the agreement
my dad had signed was no longer legal. That's when
Dad disappeared. Me and Mum were alone then.

Mum sent me to her sister's in Hackney. She stayed in
Doncaster, so she could sign on every week. She wanted
me to continue my education away from stress. I went to
the Haggerston School for Girls in Hackney for about
three months. It was good, but I missed my mum.

I went back to Doncaster after Mum applied for asylum.
It was good to be in Doncaster again, and everything for
me was kind of OK for a while. I went back to Stirling
Primary, into Year 6. But we still didn't know where Dad was.

Trouble again – 28 August, 2007

Then they took me and Mum back to Yarl's Wood. Our asylum application had been rejected. It was horrible. They took us to a police station in a black car with black windows. It was so scary. We went to the police station and then they took us in a cage van, back to Yarl's Wood.

They told us we were there because we had come through Germany. The problem wouldn't go away.

Yarl's Wood was frightening. We had to go through twenty doors to get to where we slept. Keys and doors. Clank. It was a prison. Me and Mum had one small room. There was also a sitting room for all the families. And out of the windows all you could see was huge walls. Everybody there was down except the prison officers. They could go home, couldn't they? I got so badly depressed they took me to hospital and I stayed there for a few days.

We finally got help from NCADC (National Coalition of Anti-Deportation Campaigns), from a man called John O. He campaigns for refugees. He began things for us and we got another solicitor then, too.

We stayed in Yarl's Wood for three months. I hated it.

The Nightmare at Heathrow –
November, 2007

Then on 15 November, 2007, only a week after I went to hospital, they came and got me and Mum and put us in the back of a black van. They took us to Heathrow for a flight to Germany. My mum was crying. One of the guards said to me, "You know, if you refuse to go on the plane, we'll make you; tell your Mum what I said."

Then two guards took us on to the plane. I started screaming and shouting. The pilot stopped the plane and they took us off.

We were taken back to Yarl's Wood. After a few days they took me to hospital again because of all the screaming on the plane and because I was so depressed.

While I was in hospital our solicitor told us the Home Office had hired a private jet to take us back to Germany. That's when I started to feel really strange. I was so depressed.

Then something magic happened. The Children's Commissioner, Sir Albert Aynsley-Green, came to visit me in hospital. He asked me about everything. He really listened. The next day I got out of hospital and we left Yarl's Wood.

The end of it – June, 2008

Just after my 14th birthday, we were sent to Millbank
Asylum Induction Centre in Ashford, Kent. It's not like
a prison. I started school at The Towers School.
It was great.

In February, 2008, our solicitor told us Germany had
been taken out of our case so we weren't illegal any
more. And in March we were given a house in Newcastle.
I started at Burnside Community High School then.
I loved the school. I had loads of friends. I just wanted
a normal life. Doesn't everybody?

Then our nightmare ended. Just like that. We were given indefinite leave to stay on 12 June, 2008.
My dad came back to us about then, but he left again. We don't know why.

In January, 2009, Dad came back again. He was very sick and it turned out to be cancer. He wanted to be in London next to his brothers, so we left Newcastle for my dad's sake and came here to London.

My dad died on 18 February, 2009. It's so sad. He can't enjoy our life now. He was 44 years old. It's not old, is it? And we still don't know why he disappeared. All I know is that whatever he did, he didn't do it for the wrong reason.

London and the Future – 2009

I'm happy now. That's the thing. I'm happy. My mum
still gets a bit depressed about it all. But we're together
and free.

I've just started at Gladys Aylward School in Enfield.
I like school most of the time. I'm making more friends.
I go out with them when I can. We like going to the
movies and just hanging round really. Talking, you know.
And I really like music. I like anything good,
but especially R & B.

Me and my mum also listen to Kurdish music sometimes.
It makes us a bit sad, but that's OK.

I want to be a doctor one day.
We'll see.

I just want to have a life. I want
to stay in this country. That's
what I want and now I can.
It's wonderful.

This is a picture of my mum
and me

Did you Know?

★ The Kurds are a non-Arabic people, with their own language and culture. Most are Sunni Muslims, and the vast majority speak Kurdish, a language related to Persian.

★ The Kurdish people mostly live in a mountainous area of southwest Asia bordering Turkey, Iraq, Iran, Armenia and Syria. This area is generally known as Kurdistan, 'Land of the Kurds.'

★ The population of Kurdistan is estimated to be between 30 and 40 million. About half of this number live in Turkish Kurdistan.

★ Turkish Kurdistan covers an area of about 190,000 square kilometres (118,750 square miles). The main towns are Amed, Bitlis and Van.

★ The rivers are an important part of Kurdish life and history. The most important ones are the Murat and the Buhtan. The Tigris and Euphrates rivers also begin in the Kurdish mountains and flow into Iraq and Syria, as well as supplying water for Turkey's hydroelectric power.

What happened?

The recent history of the Kurdish people is very complex, and this is just a brief outline about the Kurds who live in Turkey.

Before World War I, traditional Kurdish life was nomadic, revolving around sheep and goat herding throughout the plains and highlands of Turkey and Iran. After the war, the Allies (including France, Britain and the United States) created a number of new nation-states, and promised the Kurds an independent homeland.

However, for many complex reasons, this didn't happen. And finally, in Turkey, Kamal Ataturk, the new Turkish ruler, rejected the idea of independence for the Kurds. In the end, the Kurds were no longer as free to roam, and were forced to abandon their traditional ways. Many became farmers.

They continued to campaign for independence throughout the 1920s and 1930s, and Turkish forces brutally put them down.

By the 1970s, the Kurds had established an opposition group in Turkey called the Kurdish Workers Party (PKK), led by Abdullah Ocalan. They demanded cultural and political rights for the Kurds.

The Turkish Government refused to recognise the Kurds as a minority with special rights, and in 1984 the PKK started a guerrilla campaign. Government forces responded and there has been a fierce conflict ever since. An estimated 37,000 people have been killed during this conflict, including many women and children. Human rights groups have criticised both sides for their conduct in the conflict.

In 1999, Abdullah Ocalan was captured and imprisoned for life.

The situation for the Kurds is still unresolved.

JANETTA OTTER-BARRY BOOKS

MELTEM'S JOURNEY copyright © Frances Lincoln Limited 2010
Text copyright © Anthony Robinson and Annemarie Young 2010
Illustrations copyright © June Allan 2010
Photograph pp 20/21 copyright © Simon Jones

First published in Great Britain in 2010 and in the USA in 2011 by
Frances Lincoln Children's Books, 4 Torriano Mews,
Torriano Avenue, London NW5 2RZ

www.franceslincoln.com

A catalogue record for this book is available from the British Library

ISBN: 978-1-84780-031-2

Illustrated with watercolour

Printed in Dongguan, Guangdong, China by Toppan Leefung in May 2010

1 3 5 7 9 8 6 4 2